M000096984

Texas

INTERACTIVE

NOTEBOOK

By Carole Marsh

WORD FROM THE AUTHOR

Dear Teacher,

This book is your guide to using Interactive Notebooks for Texas state studies!

Included are hands-on, reproducible activities to teach your students about Texas geography, history, people, events, government, economics, state symbols, and more. Also included is a step-by-step guide to the Interactive Notebook concept.

Your students and you are sure to have a great time and a fabulous year, learning about our amazing state with this fun, creative, effective approach.

I'd love to hear from you on Facebook, Pinterest, or by email, and to see pictures of your students' work!

Best regards,

Carole Marsh

Carole Marsh

©2017 Carole Marsh/Gallopade All rights reserved.
Published by Gallopade • Manufactured in the USA

TABLE OF CONTENTS

WHY USE INTERACTIVE NOTEBOOKS?

Interactive Notebooks are great for students!

- Building an Interactive Notebook helps students build organization skills as they take responsibility for their learning resources.

- The Interactive Notebook provides students with an outlet to apply the knowledge they gain in ways that express their own ideas and creativity.

- Guided writing activities incorporated into an Interactive Notebook help your students develop into independent, creative, reflective thinkers.

- And, once completed, an Interactive Notebook becomes a comprehensive and engaging review tool to help your students master content and prepare for tests.

Interactive Notebooks are great for teachers!

- You can easily customize your instruction.

- You direct the learning process and pace.

- You determine where to dig deeper...and when and where to add pizzazz!

- You choose which projects to use as instruction, which projects to use as reinforcement, which projects to use as independent practice, and which projects to use as assessments.

- You can supplement activities with your own texts and projects.

- And, you meet the unique needs of your students—in each and every year!

Let's get started!

WHAT'S NEEDED FOR INTERACTIVE NOTEBOOKING?

What Students Need:

- a spiral-bound composition book (each student needs his or her own book)
  (spiral-bound books that are slightly larger than 8.5x11 are ideal for Interactive Notebooks)

- scissors, crayons or colored pencils, highlighters, glue/glue-sticks, pencils

- brad-style fasteners (needed for two activities)

- access to reference sources you approve for research
  (e.g., books in your classroom, library materials, and supervised use of Internet, per your school policy)

Remember, Interactive Notebooks will be creative and colorful, but not all students are great artists, and that's OK. The benefits of Interactive Notebooking are not in perfect coloring, cutting, and folding. They are in the interactive approach to learning; the pride students take in their work; the deeper connection they develop to the topics they study; and the creativity, mindfulness, and reflection that go into their work. In fact, gluing down a foldable, only to then realize it's upside down, is part of the learning process—and not the end of the world! So, recognize their efforts, where they shine in their own unique ways, and the learning that occurs.

What Teachers Need:

- access to a copier or printer, plus paper and toner (or a copy allowance)

- back-up supplies in case students need them

- classroom reference materials for students to use as needed

- **Just as importantly, you'll need a plan and activities that are designed for the Interactive Notebook process. *That's where we come in!***

This book provides you with an effective plan, plus loads of activities that are designed specifically to be used as part of an Interactive Notebook. You also get a variety of writing prompts, activity extensions, and reflection ideas—one or more for each activity. We've provided a "Let's Learn About Texas" get-started letter for students that explains the basic Interactive Notebooking benefits, organization, and expectations. Adapt or use as is; just add your supply list to the back. There's even a rubric for easy Interactive Notebook grading. And it's all easily adaptable and customizable in any way you choose.

HOW TO CREATE AN INTERACTIVE NOTEBOOK

Step 1: Every book needs a cover!

Students can illustrate their Interactive Notebook covers with a collage of pictures that represent Texas to them. Possibilities include the state name, a map, their own picture, sports teams, nature scenes, state symbols, or anything else they select. Students can glue pictures directly to the cover or to a separate sheet of paper that they then glue to the cover. Wrap several pieces of clear packing tape across the cover to hold it together and protect it throughout the year.

Step 2: Personalize Page One

Students should write their name, how long they have lived in Texas, what they love about Texas, and places in Texas they have visited.

Step 3: Stay organized with a Table of Contents (TOC)

Students should write "Table of Contents" on the top of pages 2-5 (or 2-7 if you plan to add supplemental material). This sets aside space for students to record page numbers and page topics as they build their Interactive Notebook throughout the year.

The activities in this book are designed as "spreads" where a left and right page are used for the same topic. You can allow students to list each spread/topic on one line of the TOC if you follow this concept.

Students should write a page number on the outside bottom corner of each page. This will make it easy for them to find a page they are looking for.

Tip: When you make an assignment, write the TOC entry on your whiteboard, and have students record it in their TOC first. That way, they can flip back for a reminder of what goes on what page.

Step 4: Kick off each unit with a KWL Chart

A good way to launch each new unit in the Interactive Notebook is for students to create a unit page that includes a KWL chart. This gives students a chance to think about the upcoming topic in advance, encouraging them to participate in class discussion. Remind students to list their unit page and KWL in their TOC.

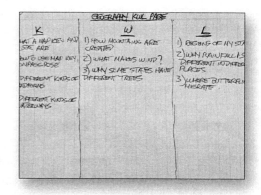

The activities in this resource are grouped into units by strand (geography, history, economics, etc.). You can adjust the order of the strands, combine strands, or move a few activities from one strand to another.

Tip: Do a notebook check soon after students create their KWLs, and you'll get insight into what students know and what they want to know, helping you customize your instruction.

Step 5: Every page deserves a title!

For any page whose activity does not include a title, students students should write a title across the top of the page. That will make it easier for them to find pages and to know at a glance what each page is about.

Tip: Build a "master" Interactive Notebook. Add activity pages as you assign them (you don't have to do them), and record extension/reflection assignments. Your notebook master will make notebook checks easy, and students can use it as a reference if they are absent or missing an assignment.

Step 6: Activities on the right ──────

Most activities and foldables are designed to fit on one page, with the other side used for writing, reflecting, and expansion activities. Votes are in, and "activities on the right" is the winner!

(The right-hand page is easier to use because it usually has flat, unused pages underneath it. Plus, because most page-flipping is right to left, glued pages adhere better to right-hand pages.)

Step 7: Expand, write, and reflect (on the left)

Make more of each learning opportunity by pairing structured activities and foldables with writing, reflecting, and expansion activities. The left-hand page of each spread is your spot for these. We've included a list to go with every activity topic, and you're sure to come up with plenty more of your own! You have a lot of flexibility in how you use this space.

Occasionally, an activity is designed to go across the top of the two-page spread (e.g., timelines). When that occurs, students can do their writing assignment underneath.

Tip: Give students a standing assignment to write a sentence about how they are impacted by what they learned. Ideas include how it changed their perspective, how they can use it, and why it matters.

Step 8: A glossary is the perfect ending!

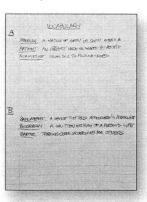

Students can build a glossary as they learn important terms throughout the year. Based on the number of pages you expect students to use in their composition books, you can suggest a reasonable number of pages for them to set aside as a glossary. Words can be listed under a letter heading in the order they are added. It's not easy to plan the right amount of space for each letter, but here are a few suggestions to help:

- 5 pages = 5 letters per page, except 6 on the last page
- 8 pages = 3 letters per page, except 5 on the last page
- less than 5 pages = not easy to alphabetize by even just one letter, but students could list key terms in the order they learn them, perhaps with unit headings for organization

Step 9: Feedback and positive reinforcement!

Show interest in your students' Interactive Notebooks to help them understand the importance of their work. Notebook checks help make sure students complete their work and make up anything they miss. A rubric at the end of this book provides a simple 10-point grading system. Feel free to customize and adapt to suit your needs. Positive reinforcement and recognition goes a long way!

Tip: Give students a copy of the rubric to put in their Interactive Notebook at the start of the year. They can use it to do self-checks throughout the year.

DETAILED ACTIVITY LIST
+ COPYING INSTRUCTIONS
& IDEAS FOR EXTENSION, WRITING, & REFLECTION
(i.e., LEFT-HAND PAGE ACTIVITIES)

Texas GEOGRAPHY

Using Maps & Globes to Learn About Texas. 15-16
(copy both pages single-sided, each on their own sheet of paper)
Tip: Display a variety of different types of state maps for students to view.
- Describe 2-3 real-life scenarios that each require use of a different map.
- A "Geographic Information System" (GIS) allows you to access many different types of geographical data, select which data you are interested in, and view it on one map. Describe a scenario where a state GIS would be useful, and explain how it would help.

My Map of Texas 17-18
(copy this activity front-and-back)
Create a Texas gazetteer of unique place names: Draw a vertical line down the center of a page. On the left side of the line, write down the names of at least 10 Texas cities, waterways, or other geographic features that have interesting or unusual names. Then rewrite them on the right side in alphabetical order.

Texas' Place in the United States/U.S. Regions. 19-20
(copy this activity front-and-back)
- Create a web diagram: Write your U.S. region in a center circle. Then write characteristics that define or describe your region in separate circles and connect them to the center.
- Research the highest point (elevation) in each state in your region. Write place names and elevations on a step diagram, from lowest to highest.

Texas Regions. 21
(copy this activity single-sided)
- You're hired!: Write a paragraph describing the region where you live for a promotional brochure aimed at attracting new residents and businesses.
- Describe the sights, sounds, smells, tastes, and feel of a Texas region, but don't name the region. Let a classmate read your description and guess the region.

Texas Climate 22
(copy this activity single-sided)
- Look up the definitions of "climate" and "weather" and write them in your glossary.
- Explain the difference between climate and weather. Then explain how they are related.
- Describe the local weather for the last week and how it affected you.

Texas Agriculture. 23
(copy this activity single-sided)
- How might weather negatively impact Texas' top crops? Create a chart or diagram to explain the cause-and-effect chain of events that could occur.
- Research other types of agriculture that are successful in Texas, and list them.

Texas Nature 24
(copy this activity single-sided)
- Write a paragraph explaining why you think it is important or unimportant that Texas have a state flower, state fish, state tree, etc.
- Research an endangered or at-risk animal in Texas. List ideas to protect it.

- Create a T chart listing advantages and disadvantages of one of Texas' transportation systems. How might new technologies solve problems? How might they create drastic changes? Predict positive and negative effects.
- Plan a trip: Use a roadmap to plan a trip to another state. List all the roads you would take to drive to the state border, starting from your home or school.

Texas HISTORY

Tip: Hand out this activity sheet periodically throughout the year, especially as you cover history. There are too many great Texasns to choose only one!
Do a creative writing project about this person. You could write a poem, a letter, a journal entry, a family tree, a 5-Ws chart, a newspaer article, a comic strip, a mini-biography, etc.

- Draw or write something in the style of art of the American Indians in Texas.
- Compare a ceremony used by your own cultural group with one used by a Texas American Indian tribe. How are they similar? How are they different?

Tip: Assign these activities together, even though they go on two spreads.
- Close your eyes and imagine being an early explorer in Texas. Open your eyes and write a multi-sensory, descriptive journal entry to describe your experience.
- Draw a compass rose in the center of the page. Next to each of the eight points, list a reason why the area that is now Texas was a difficult and dangerous place to explore hundreds of years ago.

- Imagine what it would be like as a settler arriving in Texas and meeting American Indians for the first time. Write a journal entry from your perspective. Then write a journal entry from the perspective of the American Indian you met.
- Look at a current political map of Texas. Create a gazetteer listing cities, towns, or counties named after important figures in U.S. or Texas history.

- Make a timeline of key events in the life of a fictitious immigrant to Texas from one of the two groups you researched.
- Write a journal entry as an immigrant to Texas today. What similarities do you share with immigrants of the past? How is being an immigrant easier today than 100 years ago? How is it harder?

- What do you wish someone would invent? Maybe that someone is you! Describe your invention. Explain what it would do and the benefit it would provide. How might it work? What would you name it?
- Create an acrostic using the word "Invent," listing important characteristics of inventors.
- Look up and write the definitions of "invention" and "innovation." How are they similar? How are they different? Today, they are often used interchangeably. Why?

Tip: *The next six activities can be used to study many different events in Texas history, as well as the people and places involved. You can choose which events (and people) to focus on as a class, and which to let students choose from for independent work. You can also decide when to use the timeline, cause-and-effect chart, 5-Ws brochure, or biography activity pages, as they are easily adapted to many different events.*

Texas History = U.S. History. 37-38
(copy this activity front-and-back)
● Write a journal entry as a participant in the event you selected.
● Connect an event in Texas history with an issue facing Texas or the U.S. today. What can we learn from the past that might help us resolve our problem today?

Texas Timeline 39
(copy this activity single-sided)
● Write about the connections between events on your timeline.
● Describe the period of time between two events on your timeline. What was occurring? What was life like then? Were things getting better or worse? From what perspective?

Texas History Dig Site 40
(copy this activity single-sided)
● Choose something unusual or surprising about the site you selected (or about the people who lived there). Write a tour guide script to share this information.
● Research and write the definitions of "historic," "archaeology," and "preservation."

An Important Event in Texas History. 41-42
Ideas: Corpus Christi Mission, the Alamo, JFK Assassination
(copy this activity front-and-back)
Describe how this historical event influenced future generations and Texas today. How might our state be different today had this event not occurred or ended differently?

Who Am I? Texas Edition 43
(copy this activity single-sided)
● Write a letter to the person you selected. Tell them what you most admire about them, what you found most interesting about them, and what you wish you could ask them.
● What might you one day want to be famous for? Make an action plan to achieve it.

Colorful Texans 44
(copy this activity single-sided)
● What characteristics do you think of as describing a "colorful" person? How is "colorful" positive? How could "colorful" be negative? List three ways you are "colorful."
● Describe how you contribute, or will one day contribute, to Texas.

Texas GOVERNMENT

Texas Government 45-46
(copy this activity front-and-back)
Tip: Research and discuss the process of how a bill becomes a law in Texas, as a class. Students could devote a whole spread in their Interactive Notebooks to this topic.
● Write an idea for a new Texas law. Explain who it would benefit and how.
● Draw a flowchart showing the steps for making a new Texas law, from introduction of a bill through signing the bill into law.

Texas Constitution 47
(copy this activity single-sided)
● Suggest a new right or protection to add to the Texas Constitution. Explain why it is needed today.
● Flip back and reread your idea for a new Texas law. Ask yourself, "Is it constitutional?" Explain why it is or is not. Who would make the final determination? When? How?

Texas ECONOMICS

Texas STATE SYMBOLS

(copy this activity front-and-back)

Suggest an idea for a new state symbol. Write a convincing argument for why the symbol would be a great addition and a good representation of Texas.

(copy this activity front-and-back)

- List five elements you would include in the design if the Texas state flag were to be updated today. Explain the meaning of each and why you would include it.
- Research and explain why the Texas flag is sometimes flown at half-staff. List a time and reason when it was.

(copy this activity front-and-back)

- Write the Texas state motto. Then describe what it means. Suggest a new motto, or defend the current motto as still relevant for today.
- Design a seal for yourself. Then list things you could put it on.

(copy both pages single-sided, each on their own sheet of paper)

- Texas sports fans are often passionate about their teams! List reasons people become fans of certain teams. Why are sports so popular? How does sports unite us?
- Suggest a new mascot for a Texas sports team, and draw it.

(copy this activity front-and-back)

- Write copy for an advertisement in a vacation magazine urging people to come to Texas and enjoy features for which the state is famous.
- Your cousins from out-of-state are coming to visit you. It'll be their first time in Texas! Where is the #1 place you will you take them? Why?

Tip: Give students a standing assignment to write a sentence or short paragraph about how they are impacted by what they learned. Ideas include:

"What am I really glad I learned, and why?"

"How did what I learned change my perspective?"

"How can I use what I learned?"

"How can I share what I learned?"

"What do I want to learn even more about?"

INTERACTIVE NOTEBOOK INSTRUCTIONS
LET'S LEARN ABOUT TEXAS!

Dear Students,

This year, you will create an Interactive Notebook about Texas!
You will work on a wide variety of activities as you build your Interactive Notebook. You will apply the concepts and skills we cover in class to transform Interactive Notebook activity pages into unique displays of your knowledge about our state. You will learn about Texas geography, history, people, government, economics, and symbols. You will explore what unites Texas with the rest of our nation, and what makes Texas unique. And, you will extend your thinking beyond the activities to express your opinions, apply knowledge to new scenarios, and reflect on what you learn. *It's going to be a great year!*

Organization: Here is how your Interactive Notebook will be organized. We will review this and set up these pages together in class.

Location	Page Title/Description	Page #
first 7 pages	Personalized Title Page	1
	Table of Contents	2-5
	Interactive Notebook Instructions	6
	Interactive Notebook Rubric	7
middle pages	Your Activities & Work + Unit Pages & KWLs	8-?
last 5 pages	Glossary (add words throught the year)	G1-G5

Left Page

Do This Side Second

Here you will build on and reflect on what you learn.

10

Right Page

Do This Side First

Your work on pages handed out in class will go here.

11

Interactive Notebook Requirements:

● Be sure you have your Interactive Notebook and supplies in class each day.

● Your Interactive Notebook should be neat, organized, and up-to-date.

● It is your responsibility to get and make up assignments when you are absent.

● Every time you get a new assignment, add it to the Table of Contents right away.

● Your Interactive Notebook should also be colorful and creative. Highlight and illustrate important terms and concepts. Use color to add pizzazz to your charts, timelines, and activities. You do NOT have to be a great artist to produce a great Interactive Notebook—it's the effort and learning that count.

Activity Key:
gray shading = glue
dashed line = cut
thick solid line = fold

P.S. Read instructions carefully and put care into your work, but don't panic if a paper tears, you cut the wrong lines, or you glue something upside-down. We can tape it, glue it, redo it, or just let it be upside-down—it's definitely NOT the end of the world!

INTERACTIVE NOTEBOOK RUBRIC

This rubric is based on an easy-to-use 10-point scale. Circle points earned in each category and tally at the end.

Student Name: _____ **Date:** _____

CATEGORY	GREAT JOB!	ALMOST THERE	NEEDS WORK
Notebook Organization (max 2 points)	All pages have numbers and titles. Table of contents is up-to-date, neat, and organized. Each unit begins with a KWL chart. KWL charts are updated for completed units.	Missing a few page numbers and titles. The table of contents is up-to-date, and fairly neat and organized. KWL pages are fairly current.	Missing many page numbers and titles. Table of contents is missing many entries and needs to be neater and more organized. KWL pages are missing or incomplete.
Points Earned	2	1	0
Left-Facing Page Assignments (max 4 points)	All assignments to date have been completed. Work is thorough. Writing is detailed and energetic/interesting. Writing and reflection assignments show student is thinking about what is being learned.	Nearly all the assignments to date are completed. Work is fairly thorough. Writing is generally detailed, but could be even better if more time is spent thinking about the material.	Quite a few assignments given in class are missing from the notebook or incomplete. Work needs to be more thorough. Writing needs more detail and energy. Student needs to put more time into thinking about the material.
Points Earned	4	3	1 0
Right-Facing Page Activities (max 4 points)	All activities to date are completed. Work shows creativity and thought. Research tasks show good effort and results. Writing tasks are done with good detail. Coloring, drawing, cutting, and gluing are done neatly. All required notes and labels are present.	Nearly all activities are completed. Work shows some creativity and thought but could use more effort and research. Writing is generally detailed but could be improved. Coloring, drawing, cutting, and gluing are generally good. Most notes and labels are present.	Several activities are missing or incomplete. Coloring, drawing, cutting, and gluing are sometimes sloppy. Notes and labels are missing or incomplete. More effort is needed in research, content, and creativity. Writing needs more detail and energy.
Points Earned	4	3	1 0

Total Points Earned:
(10 possible)

Additional Notes & Comments:

USING MAPS & GLOBES TO LEARN ABOUT TEXAS

Maps and globes help us find **where places are located**.
They also help us find out **what places are like**.

Different types of maps show different features and information.
Different types of maps can be used for different purposes.

globe

a round model of Earth; shows major physical and political features

political map

shows political features, such as boundaries and names of countries, states, regions, or cities

physical map

shows physical features, such as bodies of water, mountains, plateaus, etc.

population map

shows areas of high, medium, and low population (where people live)

transportation map

shows highways, roads, airports, and other transportation routes

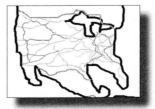

climate map

shows the climate of various areas, including temperature and rainfall

This map shows the world.

This map shows Texas counties.

This map shows Texas rivers.

This map shows how much it rains in Texas.

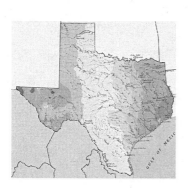

This map shows highways in Texas.

This map shows where Texans live.

This notebook activity is printed single-sided on two different sheets. Parts of each sheet will go in your Interactive Notebook.

1. Cut along the dashed lines on each page.

2. Glue the "Using Maps & Globes ..." title and text to the top of a page in your Interactive Notebook.

3. Fold along the solid lines so the maps are on the outside/top.

4. Glue the six folded maps below the "Using Maps & Globes ..." text. (Only put glue on the gray flaps. Make sure each map is face-up.)

5. One map at a time, complete the following steps:
   • Read the description on the folded map.
   • Flip up the folded map.
   • On the back of the flap, write a question about Texas that could be answered using this type of map.
   • Then, glue the <u>picture of this type of map</u> on the Interactive Notebook page underneath the flap.
   Continue until you complete these steps with all six types of maps.

Activity Key:
gray shading = glue
dashed line = cut
thick solid line = fold

MY MAP OF
TEXAS

Map Key

This is a two-sided notebook activity.
This entire sheet will go in your Interactive Notebook.

Follow these steps to complete the map on the other side of this sheet.

1. Locate and label Texas' major cities:
   - AUSTIN
   - DALLAS
   - HOUSTON
   - SAN ANTONIO

2. Which city is Texas' capital? Draw a ★ on it.

3. Draw a 😊 on the map for the city where you live. Label the city if it is not already labeled.

4. Draw Texas' major rivers in blue, and label them:
   - BRAZOS
   - RED
   - RIO GRANDE

5. Add abbreviations for cardinal and intermediate directions to the compass rose.

6. As you complete your map, create a map key to explain your symbols.

7. Create a symbol for the following physical features and add them to the map and map key.
   - GUADALUPE PEAK
   - LAKE SAM RAYBURN
   - GULF OF MEXICO

8. Double-check to be sure you did not miss any steps by finding each item on your map and crossing it off the list on this side of the sheet.

9. Glue your map into your Interactive Notebook. (Put the glue on this side of the sheet.)

REMINDER:
For all activities, gray shading indicates which part of the sheet to put glue on.

TEXAS' PLACE IN THE UNITED STATES

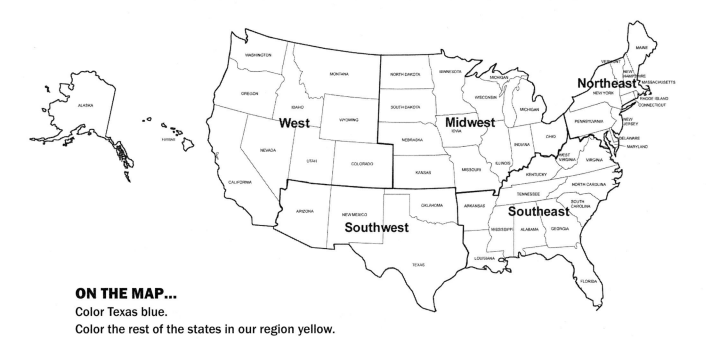

ON THE MAP...
Color Texas blue.
Color the rest of the states in our region yellow.

This is a two-sided notebook activity.
This entire sheet will go in your Interactive Notebook.

1. Fold this page in half along the solid line, so the map is on the outside.

2. Complete the activities on both sides.

3. Glue the folded sheet to the top of a page in your Interactive Notebook.
    (Only put glue on the gray flap. Make sure the map is face-up.
    The folded edge should be at the bottom.)

4. On the bottom half of your Interactive Notebook page, list characteristics
    that describe your region of the U.S.
    Include natural characteristics and human characteristics.

U.S. REGIONS

A **region** is an area with one or more common, or shared, characteristics. The shared characteristics of a region distinguish it from surrounding areas. Regions are a human construct. That means people choose the criteria by which a region is defined.

An area can be divided into regions in many ways, depending on what criteria are used. Criteria commonly used to determine regions include landforms, climate, economics, language, and culture.

The United States is commonly divided into five regions. These regions are based on shared physical characteristics and economic characteristics, as well as historical events and culture. Physical features that create natural boundaries often impact how the regions are divided.

IN THE TEXT ABOVE...

☐ Highlight the definition of "region" in yellow.
☐ Highlight some characteristics that can be used to define a region in orange.
☐ Highlight how physical features affect the way regions are defined in blue.

Texas is in this U.S. region:

FILL IN THE BLANKS...

1. A _____ is an area with one or more common characteristics.

2. Landforms and economics are _____ that can be used to define a region.

3. _____ between the regions impact how the regions are divided.

This is a one-sided notebook activity.

This whole sheet will go in your Interactive Notebook.

1. Label each region. Then lightly color each region a different color.
2. Fold along the solid line so the map is on the outside.
3. Glue the folded sheet to the top of a page in your Interactive Notebook. (Only put glue on the gray flap.)
4. Flip up the map, and write interesting facts about each region on the Interactive Notebook page underneath.

TEXAS REGIONS

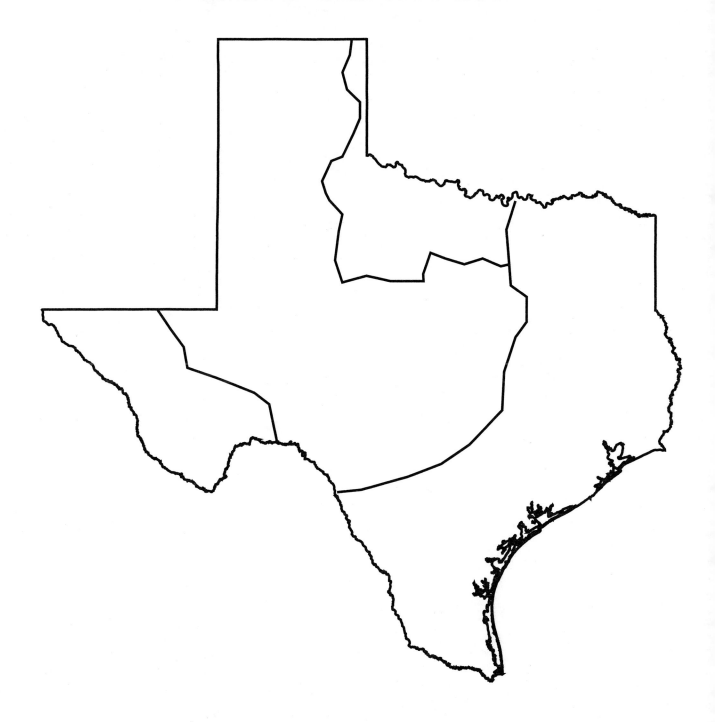

This is a one-sided notebook activity.
This entire page will go in your Interactive Notebook

1. Cut along the dashed lines.

2. Fold the page in half along the solid line. ("Texas Climate" should be on the outside.)

3. Research Texas' climate. *For example: How hot do summers in Texas get, and how cold do winters get? How much rain, sleet, or snow does Texas get each year? How long is Texas' growing season, and in which months is it? Etc.*

4. On the front of each flap, define the bold term and draw a picture to describe it.

5. Flip up the flaps and write information on the back of each to describe how Texans adapt.

6. On the sheet underneath the flaps, describe extreme weather conditions and events that Texas sometimes experiences.

7. Glue this folded sheet to the top half of a page in your Interactive Notebook. (Only put glue on the gray flap. Make sure the chart is face-up.)

8. On the bottom half of your Interactive Notebook page, create a data table. Track the weather each day for a week or month. *You can include temperature highs and lows, precipitation, wind speed, or other data.*

TEXAS CLIMATE

| Temperature | Precipitation | Growing Season |

TEXAS AGRICULTURE

How does Texas use its land and water? One way is for agriculture!
Agriculture includes growing crops and raising livestock.

Not only do we depend on agriculture for the food we eat, agriculture is essential for the production of many of our clothes, home textiles, medicines, and even automobile fuel!

This is a one-sided notebook activity.
Part of this sheet will go in your Interactive Notebook.

1. Cut along the dashed lines.

2. Fold along the solid lines. (Fold so all the flaps cover the center "Top Crops" triangle.)

3. With all three triangle flaps folded in, put glue on the back of the center triangle and glue the foldable in your Interactive Notebook. (Only put glue on the center triangle, so the flaps still open and close. The "Top Crops" triangle should be face up when you unfold the flaps.)

4. Research Texas agriculture.

5. <u>Start with the foldable unfolded.</u>
    Write the names of three of Texas' top crops, one in each triangle.
    Draw a picture to illustrate each one.

6. Flip over each flap one at a time. On the back of each flap, list 3 goods that are made from that crop.

7. On your notebook paper underneath the flaps, or at the bottom of the page, describe why each crop is successful in Texas.

Texas Interactive Notebook
©Carole Marsh/Gallopade
www.gallopade.com • Page 23

Activity Key:
gray shading = glue
dashed line = cut
thick solid line = fold

TOP TEXAS CROPS

TEXAS NATURE

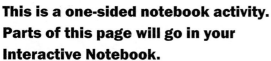

This is a one-sided notebook activity. Parts of this page will go in your Interactive Notebook.

1. Cut along the dashed lines, creating circles.

2. Fold the small circles along the solid lines.

3. Research to learn about Texas nature. *Learn about some of our abundant or unique mammals, trees, plants, fish, reptiles, etc.*

4. On the front of each small circle (the side with the gray), write the name of a different Texas plant or animal. Then draw a picture of the plant or animal on the back.

5. Glue the large circle onto the center of a page in your Interactive Notebook.

6. Glue the small circles along the outer edge of the large circle. Only put glue on the gray area, so the small circles flip open and closed. (You can glue them to open inwards or outwards—your choice!)

TEXAS TRANSPORTATION

Texas' transportation system helps move Texas resources, products, and people throughout the state, and to other parts of the nation and the world!

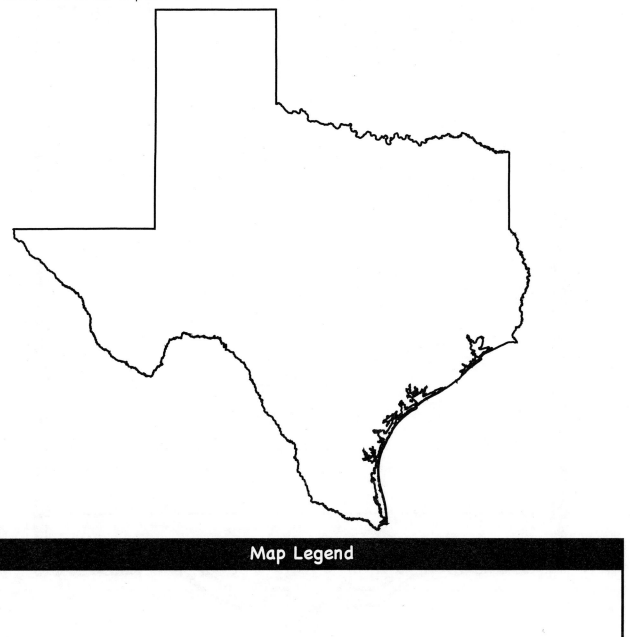

Map Legend

This is a one-sided notebook activity.

Part of this sheet will go in your Interactive Notebook.

1. On the map, mark sites and routes of important elements of Texas' transportation system. *Possibilities include interstate highways, airports, truck terminals, railroads, ports, etc.* Label the sites and routes.

2. As you draw your map, create a map legend to explain your symbols.

3. Cut along the dashed line. Then glue this page in your Interactive Notebook.

A FAMOUS TEXAN

Name: _____

Born: _____ **Died:** _____

Contribution: _____

_____

_____

_____

This is a one-sided notebook activity, but you may use it multiple times.
Most of this sheet will go in your Interactive Notebook.

1. Research a famous Texan who had a major impact on our state, country, or the world!
2. Complete the picture frame:
   • Draw, or print and glue, a picture of the person you selected.
   (Your illustration could be a portrait or it could show a scene from his or her life.)
   • Fill in the missing details. Describe the contribution made and why it was important.
3. Cut along the dashed line.
4. Glue the picture frame on the top of a page in your Interactive Notebook.
5. Below the picture frame, describe how this Texan's contribution affects your life today.

AMERICAN INDIANS IN TEXAS

This is a two-sided notebook activity. This entire sheet will go in your Interactive Notebook.

1. Fold along the solid lines to create a brochure. ("American Indians in Texas" is your cover, so it should be on top when folded. The gray section should be on the bottom.)

2. Research two American Indian groups or tribes who lived in Texas.

3. Write the names of the two groups on the front cover of your brochure.

4. On the inside panels of the brochure, describe how each American Indian group met its needs for food, shelter, and clothing. *What did they eat? How did they get it? Did they live in permanent villages or were they nomadic? How did they dress? Etc.*

5. Describe other aspects of each group's culture, such as celebrations, music, art, and dance, on the "Customs & Traditions" panel.

6. Illustrate the cover and panels of your brochure based on what you learned.

7. Glue the brochure into your Interactive Notebook. (Put glue on the gray panel only.)

Customs & Traditions

Group or Tribe:

Group or Tribe:

Food

Group or Tribe:

Group or Tribe:

Shelter

Group or Tribe:

Group or Tribe:

Clothing

Group or Tribe:

Group or Tribe:

TEXAS EXPLORATION

Francisco de Coronado was a Spanish nobleman who came to the Americas in 1535. He was named governor of a province in New Spain (today's Mexico) and used his power to stop revolts by slaves and indigenous tribes.

Francisco de Coronado began to hear stories about seven faraway cities made from gold that the American Indians called Cíbola. He wanted to conquer these cities and give their wealth to Spain. In 1540, Coronado helped pay for and lead an expedition north in search of Cíbola. The group included more than 300 soldiers, 800 Indians and slaves, and hundreds of horses, cattle, and other livestock.

The trip turned into a seven-month journey through hot desert lands. Supplies ran low, and Francisco de Coronado and his men were nearly starving by the time they found a village a priest in the party believed to be Cíbola. But there was no gold to be found there.

Francisco de Coronado sent scouts in several directions to seek the riches he wanted. They traveled down the Colorado, Arkansas, and Rio Grande rivers; and explored many present-day U.S. states starting in Arizona and New Mexico, and continuing west to Texas, Oklahoma, and Kansas. Coronado and his men faced many trials but never found gold!

Francisco de Coronado and his men are believed to be the first white men to see the Grand Canyon and the Colorado River. They explored vast areas of desolate, uncharted land covered by mountains, rivers, deserts, and forests. They claimed all the territory they explored for Spain, met new American Indian tribes, and created valuable maps.

But without finding gold, Francisco de Coronado was called a failure when he finally returned to Mexico. Later, authorities accused him of corruption and mistreating American Indians. He was found guilty and forced to leave his position in the government.

IN THE TEXT ABOVE...
- ☐ Highlight mentions of cardinal or intermediate directions in yellow.
- ☐ Highlight mentions of bodies of water in blue.
- ☐ Highlight mentions of other features, such as mountains and borders, in green.

This is a one-sided notebook activity.
Glue this entire sheet onto a page in your Interactive Notebook.

FRANCISCO DE CORONADO

This is a one-sided notebook activity.
Two parts of this sheet will go in your Interactive Notebook.

1. Cut along the dashed lines.

2. Color the illustration in the center.

3. Fold along the solid lines. (Fold flaps inward, over the illustration, so the outer corners meet in the center.)

4. Write interesting facts about Francisco de Coronado and his expeditions on both sides of each flap.

5. Glue the foldable to the center of a page in your Interactive Notebook. Glue the title above it.
   (Only put glue behind the center diamond where the picture is, so the flaps still open and close.)

Who?

Who?   Who?

Where?   When?

Why?

Texas Interactive Notebook
©Carole Marsh/Gallopade
www.gallopade.com • Page 31

This is a two-sided notebook activity.

Part of this sheet will go in your Interactive Notebook.

1. Cut along the dashed lines on the other side of this sheet.

2. Fold along the solid lines. (Fold flaps inward, over the center title.)

3. Glue the foldable in your Interactive Notebook.
    (Just put glue on the gray area, so the flaps still open and close. Be sure the title is face-up.)

Instructions continue on other side...

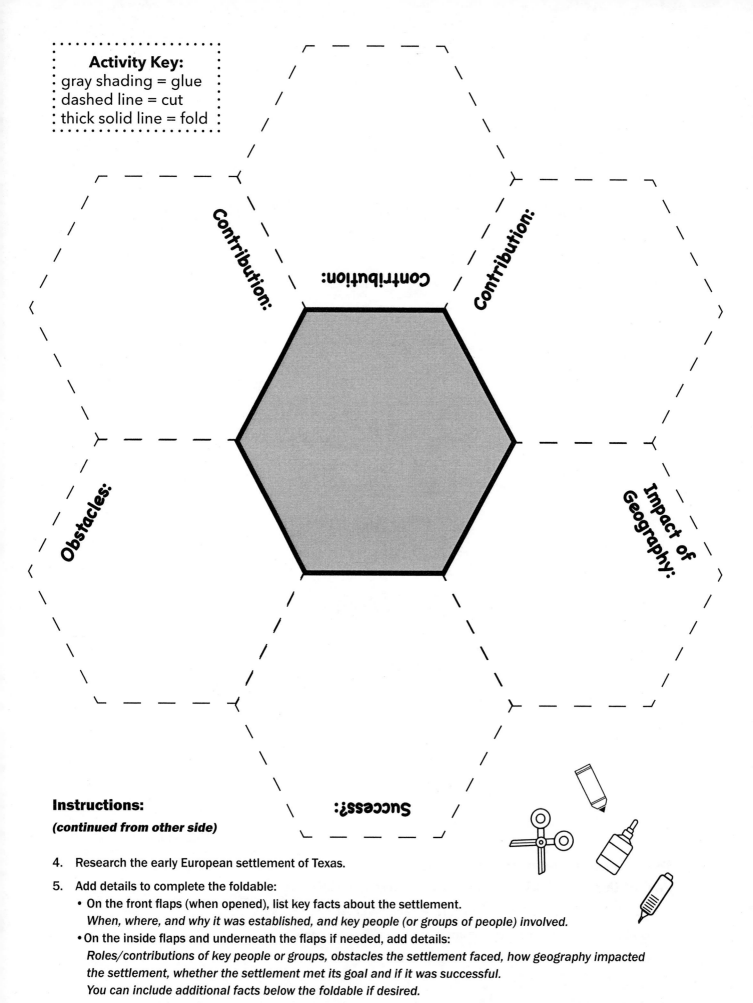

Contribution:

Contribution:

Contribution:

Contribution:

Obstacles:

Impact of Geography:

Success?:

Instructions:

(continued from other side)

4. Research the early European settlement of Texas.

5. Add details to complete the foldable:
    - On the front flaps (when opened), list key facts about the settlement.
      When, where, and why it was established, and key people (or groups of people) involved.
    - On the inside flaps and underneath the flaps if needed, add details:
      Roles/contributions of key people or groups, obstacles the settlement faced, how geography impacted the settlement, whether the settlement met its goal and if it was successful.
      You can include additional facts below the foldable if desired.

This is a two-sided notebook activity.

This entire sheet will go in your Interactive Notebook.

1. Research two of the immigrant groups that helped shape Texas history.

2. Cut halfway up the page along the two dashed lines. Stop cutting at the solid line.

3. Fold each flap over on the solid line. (The Venn diagram should be on the outside.)

4. Write the names of two different immigrant groups under "Group 1" and "Group 2".

5. Use the Venn diagram to compare and contrast the two groups. *Include details such as where they came from, where they settled, when they came, why they immigrated here, etc.*

6. Flip up the flaps. On the back of the two outside flaps describe cultural aspects of each of the two groups. *What language did they speak, what religion did they practice, what foods did they eat, and other aspects of their customs and traditions.* On the back of the center flap describe some of Texas' culture that they would have found new and different than what they were used to.

7. Under the bottom title "Texas: Our New Home," illustrate how the two groups adapted and contributed to their new home.

8. Glue this sheet on the top half of a page in your Interactive Notebook.
    (Only put glue on the gray flap. Make sure the Venn diagram is face-up.)

9. On the bottom half of your Interactive Notebook page, draw or glue a world map, and identify the countries or locations the two groups of immigrants came from. Then trace their paths to Texas.

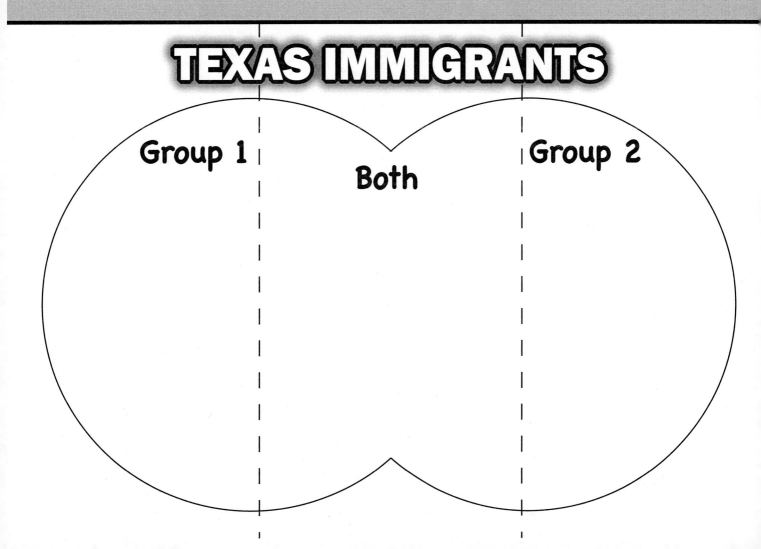

TEXAS IMMIGRANTS

Group 1

Both

Group 2

Texas: Our New Home!

Group 1
Culture

New
Culture

Group 2
Culture

TEXAS INVENTORS

Invention

Inventor

This is a two-sided notebook activity. This sheet will be cut into two pieces. Both parts will go into your Interactive Notebook.

1. Research three inventors from Texas.
    They can be from the state's past or present.

2. Cut along the dashed lines.

3. Fold along the solid lines.

4. With the flaps closed, write the name of each inventor on the left outside flap, and write the name of his or her invention on the right outside flap.

5. On the insides of the flaps, glue or draw pictures of each inventor and his or her invention.

6. On the center lines, describe the impact of each invention. *Explain who it helped, how it helped, and how it changed lives.*

7. Glue the "Texas Inventors" title to the top of a page in your Interactive Notebook.

8. Glue this foldable in your Interactive Notebook, underneath the title.
    (Only put glue on the gray section, so the flaps continue to open and close.)

Invention

Inventor

Invention

Inventor

Activity Key:
gray shading = glue
dashed line = cut
thick solid line = fold

Inventor   **Invention**

_____

_____

_____

_____

_____

_____

_____

Inventor   **Invention**

_____

_____

_____

_____

_____

_____

_____

Inventor   **Invention**

_____

_____

_____

_____

_____

_____

This is a two-sided notebook activity.

This entire sheet will go in your Interactive Notebook.

1. Select one of the events on the list, and highlight it.
2. Research to learn more about that event. Explore how Texas' people and places were involved. Think about and make inferences to determine how the event impacted Texans.
3. On the back of this sheet, describe causes, the event, and results in the center boxes.
4. In the bubbles around the event, describe how people and places in Texas contributed to this event. (You can add extra bubbles if you need to.)
5. Fold along the solid line so the list of events is on the outside.
6. Glue this folded sheet to the top of a page in your Interactive Notebook. (Only put glue on the gray flap.)
7. Flip up the sheet. On your Interactive Notebook page underneath, describe the impact this event had on Texas and the United States. *For example: What groups of people were affected by the event? How did life change during the event? How did life change after the event? What were positive outcomes? What were any negative outcomes?*

TEXAS HISTORY = U.S. HISTORY

Not only does Texas history include what happened in Texas, our state history includes the role of Texas and Texans in the historic events of the United States!

Texas has played an important role in all of these events:

- **Territorial Growth and Expansion of the United States**
- **The American Civil War**
- **Reconstruction and Change**
- **American Indian Removal and the Trail of Tears**
- **The Great Movement West**
- **Industrialization and Urbanization**
- **Building of Railroads, Highways, and Airports**
- **Immigration to America**
- **World War I and World War II**
- **The Great Depression and New Deal**
- **The Cold War**
- **America's Civil Rights Movement**
- **Women's Suffrage Movement**
- **Development of a Modern Economy**
- **Development of a Global, Connected Society**
- **& Lots More!**

RESULTS

EVENT

CAUSES

TEXAS TIMELINE

This is a one-sided notebook activity.

Part of this sheet will go in your Interactive Notebook, glued across two pages.

This activity sheet can be used for many different topics throughout the year.

1. Research an event, as instructed by your teacher.
2. Fill in the timeline squares with text and illustrations about key events.
3. Cut along the dashed lines.
4. Write a title for your timeline, across the top of the sheets.
5. Glue the timeline horizontally across the top of a two-page spread in your Interactive Notebook.
6. Your teacher will tell you what to write about underneath.

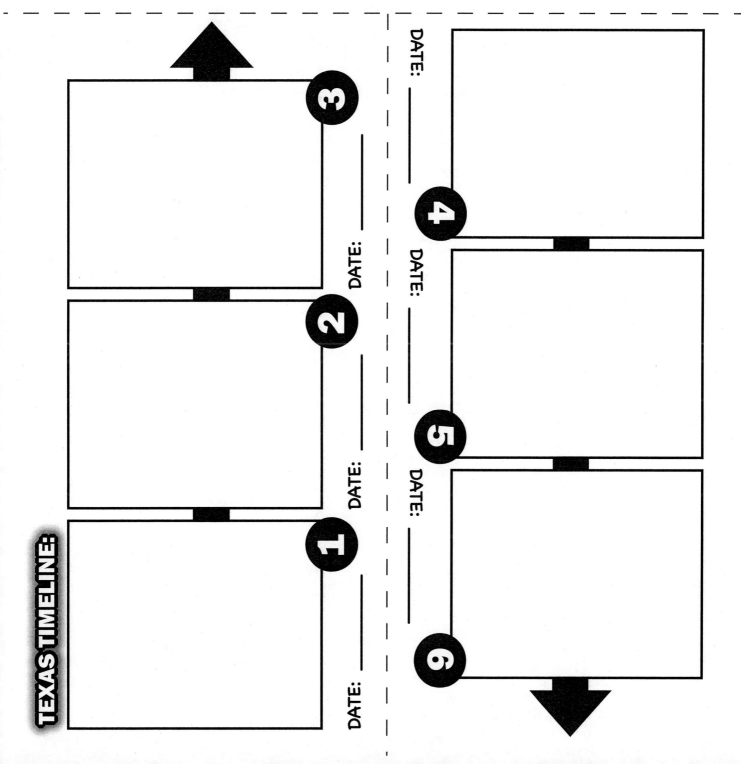

This is a one-sided notebook activity.

This entire sheet will go in your Interactive Notebook.

1. Research an archaeological site, or an old settlement or village, in Texas.
2. Write the name of the site you are researching in the dotted box.
   On the map of Texas, draw a star to show where the site is located.
   Then list facts and details about the site based on your research. Describe or draw any artifacts found.
3. Fold along the solid line so the title and facts are on the outside.
4. Glue this folded sheet to the top of a page in your Interactive Notebook. (Only put glue on the gray flap.)
5. Flip up the sheet, and on the back, illustrate what the site looked like long ago. Include artifacts that were found or could be found at your dig site. Underneath, on your Interactive Notebook page, describe what you learned about the people associated with your site. What conclusions do artifacts tell you about their way of life?

TEXAS HISTORY DIG SITE

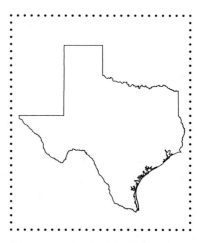

AN IMPORTANT EVENT IN TEXAS HISTORY

Who?

What?

This is a two-sided notebook activity.
This entire sheet will go in your Interactive Notebook.
You can use this activity sheet multiple times throughout the year.

1. Cut along the dashed line.

2. Fold along the solid lines.

3. Research an important event from the history of Texas. (Your teacher may assign a specific topic.)

4. Create a brochure about the event. On the five panels of the brochure, write about <u>what</u> happened, <u>who</u> was involved, <u>when</u> it occurred, <u>where</u> it took place, and <u>why</u> the event was significant. Add illustrations.

5. Glue the brochure on a page in your Interactive Notebook. (Only put glue on the gray section.)
   Glue the "An Important Event..." header above the brochure.

When?

Where?

Why?

This is a one-sided notebook activity, but you may use it multiple times.
This whole sheet will go in your Interactive Notebook.

1. Select a person from Texas whom you find interesting or whom you want to know more about.
2. Write interesting facts about this person in the picture frame—but do not write his or her name.
3. Fold along the solid line so the picture frame and facts are on the outside.
4. Glue this sheet to the top of a page in your Interactive Notebook. (Only put glue on the gray flap.)
5. Flip up the sheet. Underneath, write the name of the person, and draw or glue pictures of him/her and things related to his/her life.
6. With the frame closed flat, show your sheet to classmates to see if they can guess "Who am I?"

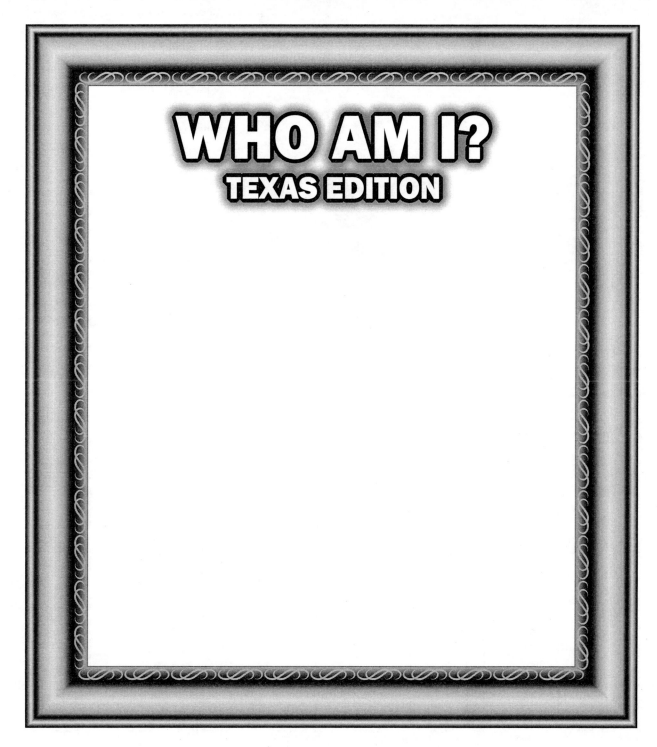

WHO AM I?
TEXAS EDITION

COLORFUL TEXANS

A **COLORFUL** Texan:

This is a one-sided notebook activity. Parts of this sheet will go in your Interactive Notebook.

1. Choose a Texas person to research. Write his or her name on the crayon box, and add an illustration of him/her.

2. Write important facts about the person on each crayon.

3. Color each crayon a different color, but only lightly color on the facts.

4. Cut along the dashed lines to cut out the box and crayons.

5. Fold the box along the solid lines.

6. Glue the crayon box in your Interactive Notebook. (Only put glue on the gray flaps. The top of the box should be open.)

7. Slide your crayons in your crayon box.

Add as many colorful Texans to this Interactive Notebook page as you like!

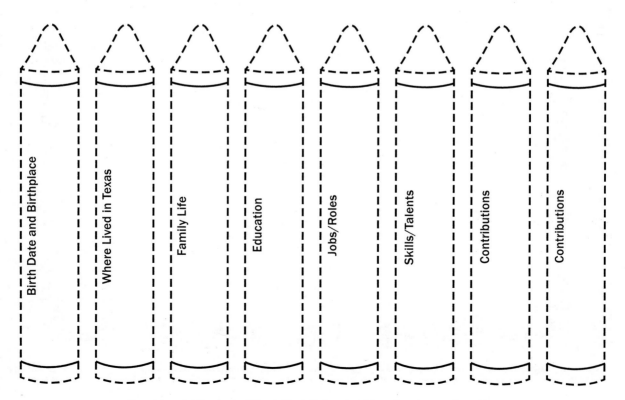

Birth Date and Birthplace

Where Lived in Texas

Family Life

Education

Jobs/Roles

Skills/Talents

Contributions

Contributions

TEXAS STATE GOVERNMENT

Executive Branch

TEXAS GOVERNMENT

Activity Key:
gray shading = glue
dashed line = cut
thick solid line = fold

This is a two-sided notebook activity.
This entire sheet will go in your Interactive Notebook.

1. Cut along the dashed lines.

2. Fold along the solid lines.

3. Research to learn about Texas' state government.

4. Decorate the front flaps of this sheet with pictures or words that represent each branch of government.

5. Open the flaps, read about Texas government, and answer the questions.

6. Glue this sheet at the top of a page in your Interactive Notebook.
   Only put glue on the gray area; do not glue the flaps.

7. Once this sheet is glued in your Interactive Notebook, list ways the Texas state government is similar to the United States federal government and ways it is different. You can write these comparisons on the page surrounding this sheet.

Legislative Branch

Judicial Branch

TEXAS' BRANCHES OF GOVERNMENT

Texas' three branches of government are established by the state constitution.

Each branch has separate, distinct powers that cannot be taken away by either of the other two branches.

Each branch depends on the others to work effectively. This division of authority is called **separation of powers.**

Each branch also has the power to prevent the other branches from overstepping their authority. This protection is known as **checks and balances.**

Texas' executive branch is led by the _____

How long is his or her term? _____

Texas has _____ branches of government.

Texas' legislative branch is called the _____

Texas' highest court in the judicial branch is the _____

Texas' highest court has _____ justices.

CURRENT TEXAS LEADERS:

Governor: _____

Lieutenant Governor: _____

Attorney General: _____

How long is the term for a state senator? _____

How long is the term for a state representative? _____

How long is the term for a justice on Texas' highest court? _____

TEXAS CONSTITUTION

The **U.S. Constitution** is one of our country's most important documents.

The **Texas Constitution** is one our state's most important documents.

Each constitution establishes a government, provides the structure for how that government operates, identifies government's key responsibilities, sets limits on what the government can do, and tells for whose benefit the government exists.

A **preamble** is an introduction. The preamble of an important document usually identifies on whose authority and for what purpose the document was created. The U.S. Constitution begins with a preamble. The Texas Constitution does too!

IN THE TEXT ABOVE...
- ☐ Highlight several ways the U.S. and Texas constitutions are similar in blue.
- ☐ Highlight one way they are different in yellow.
- ☐ Highlight a synonym for "preamble" in pink.

Preamble of the Texas Constitution

Humbly invoking the blessings of Almighty God, the people of the State of Texas, do ordain and establish this Constitution.

This is a one-sided notebook activity. Parts of this sheet will go in your Interactive Notebook.

1. Cut along the dashed lines.

2. Glue the top part of this page onto the top half of a page in your Interactive Notebook.

3. Fold along the solid line of the preamble.

4. Glue the preamble to the bottom half of your Interactive Notebook page so it is face up and can flip up. Only put glue on the gray flap.

5. Flip up the preamble. On the Interactive Notebook page underneath, explain in your own words what the preamble of the state constitution says.

6. Research how many times the Texas Constitution has been amended. Write that information on the bottom half of your Interactive Notebook page, to the side of the preamble.

I'M A TEXAS VOTER!

One day you will be old enough to vote. But first, you need to register!

STATE OFFICIAL VOTER REGISTRATION FORM

You are not qualified to vote if you have been convicted of a felony and have not received a restoration of voting rights. You may apply to the Governor to restore your voting rights.

| **Qualifications** | 1. Are you a citizen of the United States? ☐ Yes ☐ No |
| | 2. Will you be 18 years of age on or before Election Day? ☐ Yes ☐ No |

If you answered "No" to either of these questions, do not complete this form.

ID Number
Provide your driver's license, non-operator ID number, or the last 4 digits of your Social Security number if you have one.

☐ driver's license #: _ _ _ _ _ _ _ _ _ _ _

☐ non-operator ID #: _ _ _ _ _ _ _ _ _ _ _ _

☐ Last 4 digits of Social Security number: XXX – XX – _ _ _ _

☐ I do not have a driver's license, non-operator ID, or Social Security number.

Additional Information
Date of birth and sex are required.

Date of Birth (month, day, year) _ _ / _ _ / _ _ _ _

Sex ☐ Male ☐ Female

Phone and/or Email (optional)

Your Name

Last

First

Middle _____ Suffix

Address Where You Live

Street Address (include apt., lot, etc.)

City _____ Zip _____ County

If homeless or you do not have an established residence, describe where you reside:

Where You Receive Mail (if different)

Address/P.O. Box

City _____ State _____ Zip

Previous Voter Registration Information

Your name was _____

Your address was _____

Your city and state were _____ Your zip was _____

Political Affiliation (check only one)

Political Parties: ☐ Democratic ☐ Libertarian ☐ Republican ☐ No Party

Non-Party Political Organizations: ☐ Green

WARNING
If you sign this form and you know the information is not true, you may be convicted of perjury and fined up to $7,500 and/or jailed for up to 5 years.

Registrant Affidavit

I swear or affirm under penalty of perjury that:
- I am the person named above.
- I am a citizen of the United States.
- I have not been convicted of a felony (or I have received a restoration of rights).
- I am at least 17 ½ years old.
- I live at the address listed above.
- I am not currently judged by a court to be "incompetent to vote."
- I do not claim the right to vote anywhere else.

Signature _____ Date _____

This is a one-sided notebook activity.
Parts of this sheet will go in your Interactive Notebook.

1. Fill out as much of this voter registration form as you can.
2. Cut along the dashed lines.
3. Glue the title and the completed form on a page in your Interactive Notebook.

TEXAS COLLEGES

This is a one-sided notebook activity.

Part of this page will go in your Interactive Notebook.

1. Research a Texas college or university.

2. Write key facts inside the diploma.

3. Decorate the diploma, using the school colors. Sign it.

4. Cut along the dashed line.

5. Glue the diploma onto a page in your Interactive Notebook.

Create diplomas for as many Texas colleges or universities as you would like!

Diploma

Name of College:

Team Mascot:

Year Founded:

Popular Degree Programs:

Location:

Famous Alumni:

Number of Students:

_____

Signed, Possible Future Graduate

CURRENT EVENTS IN TEXAS

TODAY'S NEWS
Look what's happening in our state!

• • • • • • • • •   News reported by: • • • • • • • • •

☆☆ _____ ☆☆

_____

_____

_____

_____

_____

_____

_____

_____

- -

This is a one-sided notebook activity.

Part of this sheet will go in your Interactive Notebook.

1. Learn about current events in Texas.
2. Create your own newspaper front page by writing about one of the biggest or most interesting current events. Include the who, what, when, where, and why of the event.
3. Cut along the dashed line.
4. Glue your newspaper on a page in your Interactive Notebook.

TEXAS ECONOMICS

Goods are <u>things</u> people buy or sell to meet needs and wants.

Services are <u>activities</u> people buy or do to meet needs and wants.

Producers make goods and provide services. **Consumers** buy goods and services. Producers sell goods and services to earn income or profit. Consumers buy goods and services to meet their needs and wants. People can be both consumers and producers!

IN THE TEXT ABOVE...
- ☐ Highlight the definition of "goods" in pink.
- ☐ Highlight the definition of "services" in blue.
- ☐ Highlight the reason why producers make goods and provide services in green.
- ☐ Highlight the reason why consumers buy goods and services in yellow.

This is a one-sided notebook activity.

Parts of this sheet will go in your Interactive Notebook.

1. Cut along the dashed line above. Glue the top piece of this sheet in your Interactive Notebook at the top of a page.
2. Draw a T-chart underneath the sheet. Label one column of the chart Goods, and label the other column Services.
3. Cut out the goods and services below. As you do, glue each rectangle in the correct column of the T-chart.
4. In the blank rectangles, list other goods and services popular in Texas, and draw pictures of them. Glue those rectangles into the correct column in the T-chart too.

go to a doctor's appointment at Houston Methodist

eat two chili dogs at Frank Restaurant

read a book about Texas history

watch a play at the Paramount Theatre

spend a week at soccer camp in Plano

take a class on animation at Texas A&M

buy vegetables from a local farmer at a roadside stand

buy a hammer from Home Depot

PRODUCTIVE RESOURCES

Resources are things people can use to meet their needs or to produce goods or services. Resources are also called **productive resources**.

Three types of productive resources are frequently used to produce goods and services:

Natural Resources   Human Resources   Capital Resources

A fourth type of productive resource combines the other resources to produce goods and services. This resource is known as: **Entrepreneurship**

❶ **Natural resources** are resources that occur naturally (in nature) and can be used to meet needs or to produce goods and services. They are usually found in, on, or around Earth. Examples include trees, minerals, water, and fertile soil. Climate, animals for hunting, and fish in rivers and oceans are also natural resources.

   Example: Natural resources of iron and coal are used to make steel, which is used to make cars.

❷ **Human resources** are the time and effort people spend to make goods or provide services. Human resources include the training, talents, and skills people use. Human resources are both physical and mental. All goods and services include human labor.

   Example: The labor to design a restaurant and the labor to build it are human resources.
   So is the labor to cook the meals, serve the customers, and wash the dishes.

❸ **Capital resources**, sometimes called capital goods, are items that are used to produce other goods and services, but that do not become part of the good or service produced. These include machinery, tools, and buildings.

   Example: A grocery store building as well as the racks, refrigerators, cash registers,
   and other equipment used in operating the grocery store are all capital resources.

❹ **Entrepreneurship** is also an important productive resource. Entrepreneurs combine resources to produce goods and services. Entrepreneurs take risks to bring new ideas to the market, in hopes of earning a profit. Entrepreneurs make decisions about what to produce, for whom to produce, and how to produce. They decide how to use the other resources.

   Example: A toy store owner is an entrepreneur.

IN THE TEXT ABOVE...

- ☐ Highlight the definition of "natural resources" in orange. Underline examples in orange.
- ☐ Highlight the definition of "human resources" in yellow. Underline examples in yellow.
- ☐ Highlight the definition of "capital resources" in blue. Underline examples in blue.
- ☐ Highlight the definition of "entrepreneurship" in pink. Underline examples in pink.

This is a one-sided notebook activity.
Glue this entire page in your Interactive Notebook.